SOUNDINGS

SOUNDINGS

DAVID GONZALEZ

A PUBLICATION OF THE POETRY BOX®

Editing & Book Design by Shawn Aveningo Sanders
Cover Design by Robert R. Sanders
Author Photo by Carl Cox

ISBN: 978-1-956285-24-6
Library of Congress Control Number: 2022911392
Printed in the United States of America.
Wholesale Distribution by Ingram Group

Published by The Poetry Box®, October 2022
Portland, Oregon
https://thepoetrybox.com

To all who push the edge, and find it

CONTENTS

Nuyorican

All Aboard	13
Loud as the Squeal of the F Train	14
I Come From	16
El Barrio	19
The Blade is True	21
Café con Leche	22
The Ceiba Tree	24
Eight Million Dreamers Dreaming	26
Chevy Lime Green	27
The Cross Bronx	28
Wall Mural	30
Tío Anibal	31
This Round of Life That Joins Us	32
Reluctant Archer	33

Rings of Fire, Ice, and Jazz

You/I	37
The Blue Guitar	38
Give Me a World of Art	39
Angel Dust (a fantasy)	41
Jazz Is	42
Play the Line, Orpheus	45
El Ritmo de Yankeelandia	46
Woman of Sorrow	48
Your Glance Scatters Seeds	49
Baraka's Mouth	51
Be Beatrice	53

Entanglement

Entanglement   57
Fool's Proof   58
Recipe for Blood   59
XTC   60
Multiverse   61
How the Making Happens   64
Your Footsteps   65
Wanted to Know   66
This Fury   67
Between Us   68

Above, Below, In Between

There is a Universe Growing in My
    Basement   71
I Speak for the Living Earth   72
Silent Dialect   75
White Dots/Black Void   76
Eclipse   77
Tides   78
Starfish   79
BangFlash   80
Into the Night Air   81
Life Code   82
The New Green   84
Send Yourself into the Air   85
Social Ecology   86

Back to the Beginning

My Beckoning   91
Trajectory   92
This New World   93

The Miracle of Our Near Space   94

Crazy Woman Creek Canyon   95

Eagle Cliff   96

Body World   97

Kilimanjaro   98

Krishna's Rice   99

To Breathe and Breathe   100

Spins the Wheel   101

Rest, My Warriors   103

Dead Sea   104

Isabela   105

The Rose of Mercy   106

Gathering Waters   109

Acknowledgments   111

Early Praise for *Soundings*   113

About the Author   115

About The Poetry Box°   117

NUYORICAN

ALL ABOARD

The trains keep chugging,
I get on yours,
you jump on mine,
there is no destination listed
just the track laid out in front of us
disappearing at the next turn
and over the next hill,
there is no guarantee of a smooth ride,
only that we'll move along,
some passengers hop on for a short stretch
some stay on, their heads on our shoulders
resting from all the stories,
a marching band stomps down the aisle,
then a swashbuckling pirate
and parade of three girls in yellow sundresses,
all come and all go,
the world passes by,
the train moves on,
going who knows where,
In circles? To heaven?
To nowhere at all?
I am there,
you are there,
our heads bobbing,
wide-eyed to it all,
our fingers intertwined.

LOUD AS THE SQUEAL OF THE F TRAIN

I release myself to you, New York
I release myself to you the way lovers relinquish their sanity
the way seabirds ride the wind,
I release myself to you, New York,
to fuel your fire,
to burn my outer skin
and find the new growth beneath.
I release myself to you, New York, for my discovery,
for your glory.

This New York, this asopao, minestrone, wonton, gumbo stew,
the New York beneath our feet,
the New York beside us,
in the turban,
in the dashiki,
pierced,
buttoned-down,
opened-up New York,
as smooth as the firehouse pole,
hidden as the crucifix tucked into the hoodie,
New York, mixed up and merry as a Korean salad bar,
open as the door to the library,
closed as a Wall Street vault,
loud as the squeal of the F train,
silent as downy dawn at Jamaica Bay,
gleaming as sixteen steel drums parading down Nostrand Avenue on
    Carnival Day,
gritty as the growl of a pit bull,
start spreading the news,
'cause if you're gonna make it here
first learn that the only real foreigner
is your own murky shadow,
and that the light that shines twenty-four hours a day
has the power to illuminate your soul.

Welcome to New York,
city of dreams,
the city that never sleeps won't bat an eye,
won't lower a lash,
lest we miss the minor miracles that guide us
through the cyber-streaming matrix,
and plain simple living
of our here and now.
Welcome to New York,
the magnificent location of our mortal unwinding.

I COME FROM

1.

James Baldwin said, "If you know from whence you came, there is no
limit where you can go."

I come from the Bronx, the 6 train, stickball, stickups, selling
scorecards at Yankee games,

I come from Lupita and Manolo,
She from Tiffany St., Bronx, USA, English at school, Spanish at
home, tar beach, the university of the streets,
He from Santiago de Cuba, light-skinned privileged playboy,
Saturday nights at the Tropicana partying straight through to
Sunday morning Mass.

I come from a broken couple.

I come from a happy home.

2.

I come from rivers of migration—Arabian, Iberian, European,
Indian, African.

I come from Lauriano and Bertha, my Cuban grandparents,
Catholics, merchants, they gifted grenades to Fidel and the
mountain rebels and thought of Spain as their spiritual home.

I come from Rafael and Lupe, country folk from Puerto Rico, a
barman and a seamstress who landed in the Bronx, survived the
winters, and pieced pennies together to buy a car, a house, a life.
She, broad-nosed with cinnamon skin; he, broad-shouldered with a
shock of jet-black Basque hair.

3.

I come from Coltrane—A Love Supreme,
From Wes Montgomery and Jimi,
From Leonard Bernstein and Bach,
I come from Machito, Tito Puente, Larry Harlow, the Fania All-
  Stars,
I come from Alvin Ailey,
I come from Hieronymus Bosch, Goya, Kandinsky, Picasso,
I come from Rumi, Tennyson, Galway Kinnell, Miguel Algarín,
  Sekou Sundiata,
I come from Joseph Campbell, Eduardo Galeano, Abraham Maslow,
  Robert Johnson, Maxine Greene,
I come from teachers rooted to the earth,
Hearts with the people,
Minds filled with possibilities.

4.

I come from saints and sinners, each left their mark,
I come from generations of dreamers.

I come from the sixties—those bell-bottoms rang out
(sing) "love between my brothers and my sisters, all over this land..."

I come from being a Catholic, a yogi, a clairvoyant, a nihilist, a
  mythologist, a phenomenologist;
now I just want to breathe.

[. . .]

5.

I come from the past,
I come from the future,
I come from the soil,
from carbon atoms,
from electrons orbiting at light speed,
from the graceful trajectories of quarks and uncertainty,
I come from the snap of a finger long, long ago.

El Barrio

Bring on the clave Tito Puente-style,
bring on two-three *ritmo* magic,
vaya papi que tu mambo moves me,
vaya mami que tu mirada mirrors my own curiosity,
vaya la clave,
vaya el sacred groove *que me tiene* floating *y flotando,*
and planted into the bedrock *de esta tierra firme,*
of this, our earth.

The winged clave,
uprooted, sold-out,
and chained to the miserable hold of a Portuguese slave ship,
forced into migration,
this sacred syncopation
mixed with the strains of Andalusian canto
in the sugarcane fields of El Caribe,
and landed at this spot,
this town,
this Nueva York,
El Barrio,
El Barrio, el fingertip grip onto the American dream,
where half the streets open wide to the horizon,
and the other half are dead ends,
y donde el ritmo no tiene fin,
and the groove is deep.

El Barrio, where milk is not milk—but *leche,*
where *manteca* is *manteca,*
where the plantains are *maduros,*
ripe, sweet, brown smiles.

El Barrio, where the WhatsApp call,
la llamada a tu pueblo is fricken *free,*
Grandmother's voice is honey
and you need it to be.

[. . .]

Listen, *Abuela*, in Puerto Rico, Cuba, Santo Domingo, Mexico y
    Honduras,
los muchachos eh—speak English at school,
pero español en la casa,
el lenguaje de nuestra sangre—our blood tongue at home,
and each morning I recite for them your prayer, *Abuela;*
que Dios te cubre con su santo bendición,
may God surround you with his sanctified blessing,
and then they cross themselves and go outside,
and cross themselves again when they pass the storefront churches
where the Charismatic Pentecostals are raising the roof,
and once again at the corner of 176th and Amsterdam,
where gladiolas, lilies, and everlasting silk rose blossoms
mark the spot where Papo was shot,
his lifespan "June 14th, 2000 – June 2nd, 2018, R.I.P."
spray-painted onto the tenement bricks,
and scrawled beneath the sad youthful eyes of Jesus on a plastic gold
    crucifix are the words
"Why do the good die young?"

I'm gonna move to Puerto Rico when I retire,
I'll get a house near the beach
and eat mangoes all day,
but, hey, then my kid'll probably go to college *(que Dios le bendiga)* in
    Ohio,
marry a sweet, smart girl from there,
y entonces los nietos...the grandkids will need me
and I'll need them to know where they come from,
who we are,
and how we live,
so I'll stay here in El Barrio,
life is that way,
life is that way,
moving and changing like the crackle and burst of Tito's timbales,
moving and changing
in El Barrio.

THE BLADE IS TRUE

Every walk in the woods was a hunt for Excalibur.
We went in empty-handed,
then loaded our arms with daggers, foils, blades, and axes.
This world is full of surprises/magic/blood,
at five you knew this
and readied yourself for sudden oblique attacks.

The phallic forest,
each tree penetrating the earth,
each trunk entering the sky,
each fallen branch and twig a precious gift from the fertile mystery,
with these swords in your hands
and crooked spears tucked into your belt
you became a little warrior
prepared to face whatever danger or evil would come.
When your mother and I arrived home with your newborn sister
you wore a cape, had a knife, scowled,
observed,
and relented.

Now you are a man,
your sword reshaped into the body of a violoncello
with taut sinews and a dark void that offers radiance
to the touch of your bow.

Sword, shield, body, bow,
silence, song, innocence, light,
this is your arsenal,
the forest remains,
there is no path,
the demons are real,
the blade is true.

Café con Leche

Café con leche,
brown as the earth Grandma left
when she packed her sewing skills
and came to New York in the twenties.

Café con leche,
Café Bustelo,
we knew the brew,
even as kids we knew what it could do;
sanctifier of meetings,
it made the tongue loose and loving.

Café con leche,
the wine of the kitchen altar,
flavor that guides life
directly and correctly
back to the sensuous.
This much I know.
Near forty I received the sugar bowl
from my childhood kitchen table.
A gift from both my parents,
upon their reconciliation
after thirty-five years of tense estrangement.
It has two frail handles,
and the imprint of a Cuban silversmith.
Broad, weathered, and worn,
this urn carries the nineteenth century
forward to me.
It has two handles
and inside there is a dark silence waiting.
I fill it with a hissing stream of fine cane sugar
(Domino, of course, for the sport of my people),
a rolling, pouring mountain of pure candy,
a stirring sweetness that tunes my *café con leche*
to the impossibly faint,
but undeniable,

lullaby of a happy young couple—Havana 1956,
peering down at their cooing curly-haired boy.

Finally, this bird was re-winged;
I own this bowl—
and fly.

THE CEIBA TREE

The Ceiba tree drops roots from its branches,
its smooth gray bark grows out and reaches
to surround these new shoots
and include them into the trunk,
like the place above the wrist
where ligament and vein expose their fragile weaving
beneath the translucence of skin.
In Quebradillas, Puerto Rico, there are a pair of thick ancient Ceiba
    trees
living on the narrow grass divider
between the eastbound and westbound arteries
of Ruta Dos.
Their canopy shades the comings and goings
of San Juaneros, campesinos, retirees, locos,
turistas, and second-generation Nuyoricans like me
who hunger for a bit of the island's dirt,
and a taste of our own history.

In 1927 a branch split off my family tree when
Lupe y Rafael left Borinquen to grow their leaves
in the pastures of New York City.
Trees *do* grow in Brooklyn and the Bronx,
though the seedlings have to fight their way
through the cracks in the cement
and learn to dance quickly
to avoid the heel-falls that shake the pavement all around.
Sunlight insists through the shadow filters of fire escapes,
power lines, and the high silhouettes of the tenements,
and does nurture,
does warm,
does guide the eyes to the heavens.
This branch prospered and now their great-grandchildren visit the
    Spanish language as they would any other.
Their grandchildren, now middle-aged, negotiate the waters between
    islands of safety and risk.

Their children are pensioners who are happy to watch the sunset from
   any horizon.

But in Isabella, Quebradillas, y Charcas
the roots remain intact
and in touch with the limestone earth
that erodes the landscape into sky-reaching verdant hills
and obscure valleys,
which are the wombs of histories,
where "once upon a time" and "forever after"
are born of each other.

The church that my great-great-grandfather built
on the edge of the family farm still stands,
a sign welcoming parishioners,
"Misa domingo a las once,"
is painted in rough pink letters against a background of pale blue;
the silent crucifix on its roof calls attention to the sky.

At each cousin's house I am welcomed with rice and beans,
mangoes, oranges, rum,
stories, and sepia-toned photos.
With each loving word I drop roots,
with each gripping hug I drop roots,
with each stroking hand I drop roots,
I drop roots that are embraced by the brown coffee skin
of my family,
Jochi, Elisa, Francis, Ernesto...
who stayed close to the Ceiba trees
and know the secret of their wrappings.

Eight Million Dreamers Dreaming

Listen to the talk
of the city,
listen to the talk
listen to the talk
listen to the sound of eight million dreamers dreaming
dreamers dreaming
dreaming in the city.
Listen to the talk.
How do you say "Sit with me under the Brooklyn sky"
in the 146 dialects of the city?
Listen to the sigh and moan of the neighbors' night-play,
the hiss of the kneeling bus,
the evening news,
the endless silent murmur from Green-Wood Cemetery,
the cash-box bell,
Mr. Softee's song,
the flame-chasing sirens of the FDNY,
the blues, the bop, pop, house, merengue, y salsa dura,
we are the world,
"Please stand clear of the closing doors,"
shuffling cards,
a three-point swish,
the bark of a dog,
"But, baby, I do love you"
beeps on the EKG,
beeps on the EKG,
you and me and you and me and you and me.

CHEVY LIME GREEN

Green says too little,
Spanish moss silver-white-green,
newly unfurled fern green,
yellow palm-stalk green,
the green that was burnished brown beneath the leafy canopy at
   Abuela's cousin's house in Charcas, Puerto Rico,
the one held up on stilts to stave off floods and night crawlers,
the house whose windows were ever open
because they held no panes.
There is 1959 Chevy lime green,
brightened by Caribbean sun stars bouncing off the chrome,
Cousin Chucho spread-eagled on the roof,
fingers wrapped tightly into the cab gripping the cream-colored
   ceiling upholstery on both sides,
his voice bolting with laughter,
kicking out a wild thunder that rattles my five-year-old head.
A storm of taunts and warnings consume the air,
"¡Bajate de ese carro!"
"Get off that car!"
Who-knows-who in the driver's seat floors it.
We dash out,
burning down the jungle's dirt road,
flying away.
Chucho roars with a lusty laugh,
and I am pressed into the white leather crease of the back seat,
wide-eyed and wondering
whether terror and ecstasy would forever be inseparable portions
of this life.

THE CROSS BRONX

The blackened canyons
of the Cross Bronx Expressway
solid still,
after Europe, Korea, Da Nang,
and the assassinations of the sixties,
solid still after trickle-down-to-a-dry-choke economics,
after Watergate and Contragate,
after Lindsay, Beame, Koch, Dinkins, Giuliani, and the rest,
after Grenada, Somalia, Desert Storm, and Afghanistan,
still the blackened canyon walls of the Cross Bronx hold,
hold back the crush of Jerome Avenue,
Webster Avenue,
and the Grand Concourse,
and the weight of the el,
holding back the push of Pepe 'n Papo,
holding with brick on bedrock.

Y'know Bronx homies are the craziest,
lined up at the fences looking down
to the traffic crossing town,
out past Bruckner to 95 North,
from the House that Ruth built, baby,
to the Yankee world of New England's
white clapboard and black shutters
(and they do shut tight)
on the sight and sounds
from West Farms and the Bronx River projects.

The George Washington Bridge to America
is all tied up, corrupt,
and the toll is too high for too many.
So they stay with el Bronx
tattooed onto their lives,
and the shadow-canyoned Cross Bronx cleaves,
leaves lungs scarred by exhaust
and itchy, burning eyes that water
for freedom.

But this is no land of the free,
no sea to shining sea,
this is the Bronx,
and the homies and jibaros be lined up,
watching from the overpass,
thinkin' "To what worlds are they all bound?"
"To what worlds are they bound?"

WALL MURAL

I remember when you painted the living room wall in our Bronx
    apartment,
you gave it a coat of white,
then worked for a week to paint a Greco-Roman coastal scene,
 complete with clouds, cliffs, and broken columns,
an illusion of the infinite sea,
and beyond the scene our blank wall remained
now transformed from an opaque void
into a vista that invited a voyage.

Just like that the flat wall burst open to the horizon.
Grandma was cooking in the kitchen,
the kids were running every which way,
bills had to be paid,
the old VW had an oil leak,
and you, with a bristle brush and paint, standing on a stepladder,
reaching way up to add an extra splash of gold
to the setting sun.

TÍO ANIBAL

Tío Anibal,
eres blanco y negro santo,
fumando tu tabaco
y haciéndome las bendiciones Yoruba.
Me metiste Elegua y Chango
con tus humos y cantos,
y hoy los celebro
y los entretengo,
con vivo en este ahora
con ellos rumbando
por mi ser,
como el spiral de tu inspiración
y expiración,
como tu humo
y como los gestos
de tu propia biografía.

Tío Anibal, you are a dark and light priest,
Smoking your cigar,
Chanting the African blessings,
You gave me the Yoruba spirits of Elegua and Chango,
They dance through the here and now of my being,
Like the curl of your smoke
And the gestures of your biography.

This Round of Life That Joins Us

Mother, it is the winter of your years,
and the autumn of mine,
the children match the season,
everything with them is bud and blossom,
their children are yet dreams,
your parents are present as fleeting, fragrant memories.
This round of life that joins us
is the miracle you brought me into;
with it comes the silent dawn
and the crashing wave,
the gray storm at the horizon,
and the astonishing iridescence of a blue butterfly.
All this we share as people of the earth,
I owe it to you,
You owe me nothing,
forever the scales will tip toward you,
the best I could do is pass it along,
that the stream of gratitude and wonder may continue to nourish,
that the seeds you laid into the soil bear their fruit.

RELUCTANT ARCHER
~after Kahlil Gibran

What if the archer is reluctant to release his arrow?
What if he can't let go?
What if he remembers the oak branch from which he carved it,
the stone from which the head was shaped,
the bird that sacrificed its feathers,
the sinew threads that make it one?

What if he pulled the bowstring
and the strain of it
broke open his heart,
so that memories flooded his eyes
and he was blinded by a hundred regrets
and the tenderness of an iris?

What if he looked for a target
but the horizon was all shades of purple and gold with
rays of sunlight from beyond the curve of the planet;
would he let go if he could not see more than this?

Child, you are my arrow,
I, the reluctant archer releasing you.
Tethered by imagination
to the arc of your adventure,
like the tail of a shooting star
chasing the light.

RINGS OF FIRE, ICE, AND JAZZ

You/I

You are the tear and the eye,
You are the cloud and the sky,
You are the skin and the snake,
You are the heart and the break.

I am a clown with the nose,
I am a lover fully clothed,
I am a drummer without time,
I am a poet without rhyme.

THE BLUE GUITAR

~after Wallace Stevens

The blue guitar strains to be heard,
tears slip from its sound-hole,
its grief and jubilance are quiet
and close to the wood;
you have to make a choice to risk everything
to get close to the grain
to hear it.
The blue guitar's strings quiver with fine truth,
and those who hear these tones know
that they too must sing out,
whether they are heard or not.

GIVE ME A WORLD OF ART

Two bad plaids, side by side.
Functional gestures.
Gray cinder block.
No sound.
No singing.
No metaphors.
No rhymes.
No stories.
No *once upon a times.*
No *forever afters.*
No.

Give me something with snap,
something to wake me up,
something to make me take notice.
Plaids side by side?
No, no, no.
Give me a look at the deeper you,
put it together shade by shade.
Cinder block?
Never! I want graceful spaces where my wings can unfold,
where I can fly.
Functional gesture?
No.
Show me the language of fingers and shoulders,
make this place sacred with swirling bodies.
No sound?
No singing?
Stop it!
Give me tones drunk with flavor,
rhythms rooted to the seasons,
songs saturated and soaked with meaning.
No metaphors, no rhymes,
no stories, no *once upon a times,*
no *forever afters?*
No. I would sooner die.

[. . .]

Teach me from the torch-lit stories,
so that I can see into me,
and into you,
and into our future.
Teach me with the wine of poetry
how time melts away and love remains.

Give me a world of style,
of substance,
of sensuous spirit,
a world of art.

Angel Dust

~a fantasy

Ronnie, just released from Kings County Psych after a two-week Angel Dust binge, in a Thorazine haze, blankly stares at the dank vinyl couch in the group therapy room.

Ooooh, what a little angel dust will do. How it makes the mind spin, tosses off the moorings, whirlpooling down and up into and out of this abyss and that abyss, and out into the air for a breath, and a puff, and cross-eyed breathless, and uh...oh, and uh...yes, spinning into everything under my control of absurdities laughing, not even God— or maybe me and God can do this and that, breathless smoke, and give it to me again and again, roll it up yo', spice up the spliff, sprinkle a magical milky-way onto the joint, make the hooch holler with the POWer, this is the dust of creation, and I am making myself into, I don't know, some kind of moving in and out of air, sparkling breathless. Did you see that, did you see, smoke signals puff-a-puffin' messages, oracles coming from out of my skin, this angel dust is like from the wings of angels, like from a butterfly's wings, but angels' wings, this dust has homing instincts for heaven.

Where's the joint?

Where's the joint?

Where the hell is the goddamn joint!

Jazz Is

Jazz is...

an American song
born from the mixed-blood marriage of tragedy and transcendence,
consecrated by a ring of hope.

Jazz is...

The Vanguard, 2 a.m.,
Maestro Chucho Valdes at the piano,
deconstructing a Chopin prelude into swinging post-bop chromatics
laid down upon a graceful Guangancó
and bringing us back again,
smiling, wiping sweat from his brow—
hey, it's hard work lifting a crowd to heaven.

Jazz is...

David Murray biting down on his horn,
one eye closed, the other looking skyward, searching,
making his golden snake wriggle and writhe,
riding its scales,
hissing through its vertebrae,
burning and changing skins,
sacrificing, he offers his breath,
with roaring rumble,
pops, squeaks,
overblown bolts split top to bottom,
toe to skull.
Murray blows sanctified tone
into the spaces he carves out
in the ear,
the head,
and the heart.

Jazz is...

Dizzy's "Cubana Be, Cubana Bop,"
with Chano Pozo as emissary from the island,
transporting the rhythm-magic of its waters
within the grooves of his conga,
pouring ancient 6/8 libations
into the swinging sharp 9s and augmentations,
making something new.

Jazz is...

Diz is
and will always
be...
...bop hailing down
from the heavens ce soir,
dressed in minor sevenths
and tri-tonal aura,
all aglow,
playing in mad eonic swing time,
scat scattering lightning riffs,
it's kindling for wonder,
kindling for wonder.

Jazz is...

The Vision Festival, pushing the limits downtown
early each summer,
Taking chances,
Being true to the spirit of innovation,
Giving voice to the new,
Bringing the house down and back on up with
William Parker & The Little Huey Creative Orchestra,
A festival with vision.

[. . .]

Jazz is...

Bobby Sanabria in a trance behind the traps,
Channeling bata drummers from Matanzas,
Classic clave, Boricua bomba, Buddy Rich, and Tony Williams,
Sticking it to the skins,
Releasing an incantation,
Standing between the worlds,
Riding on the traditions he is dedicated to.

Jazz is...

The American Dream,
Four walls made of rhythm and rhyme,
Floorboards hardened by the blues,
Roof raised by divine inspiration,
Doors that hinge on flow.

Play the Line, Orpheus

Play the line, Orpheus
(*scat bop lick here*)
walk the line, Orpheus,
between night and daylight.
Draw the line, Orpheus,
there in the dirt where Eurydice fell away from you.
Draw it straight and narrow,
an arrow directing you to the shadows
of your own neglected closet,
the forgotten threads of your life hang there,
the parts excluded from the 'you' you did not want to see;
suits with pockets full of forgotten promises,
pants pleated with memories,
old shoes, sour and decaying,
rooting into the soil of the dark earth,
the dark earth yet unknown,
the dark earth that is your own,
that knows your step,
your dimensions, and weight.

EL RITMO DE YANKEELANDIA

Duke Ellington, Benny Goodman, Louis Armstrong,
you can't hear music like this innocently,
it finesses its way into your neural firings,
making them burst and clap in 4/4 swing time,
your heart skips a beat to catch up,
and it never lets go.
That's jazz for you.
In Santiago de Cuba, 1941,
the golden days of the light-skinned Cuban elite,
before they lost everything to Fidel
and the mixed blessings of the Revolution,
my father, Manolo,
his cousin, Rene,
and the boys from the Club Atlético
tuned their radios to the Voice of America
to hear her stomping at the Savoy,
to snap their fingers
and bop their heads
to Artie Shaw, Cab Calloway, Gene Krupa, and the Dorseys.
I Know a Gal in Kalamazoo,
Pennsylvania Six Five Oh,Oh,Oh!
The splash of cymbals and the thump of the bass
was too much,
they had to do something,
anything, to touch it,
to be part of the scene,
to make this music their own.
With this desire
El Ritmo de Yankeelandia
was born on CMCU.
Farmacia El Salvador,
Funeraria Libertad, and Cine La Gloria,
each bought a minute or two of airtime,
just enough to pay the rent to the station,
to buy the latest 78s,
and a couple of music magazines from New York.

From 1:30 to 2:00 p.m. five days a week,
the boys took turns spinning sizzling plates
during their lunch breaks from high school,
playing the hot new releases,
being the first ones to electrify the airwaves
with the hits that had a whole generation hopping,
and which kept the young DJs hoping that one day
they would be there,
live,
in the shelter,
and the storm,
of the Big Band sounds
that were *El Ritmo de Yankeelandia.*

WOMAN OF SORROW

-after Rodin's Fallen Caryatid Carrying a Stone

Burden-borne woman of sorrow,
of long spine and strength,
you bear the heavy stone,
it is the weight of your blood path,
the weight of the patriarchy,
and the grief necessary to make this earth of troubles
into a home.

YOUR GLANCE SCATTERS SEEDS

~AFTER OCTAVIO PAZ

Your glance scatters seeds,
They jump at the asking of your eyes,
It is their reason for being, that moment of springing
outward.

~AFTER CARLOS FUENTES

When we exclude, we betray ourselves,
Generations of immigrants, itinerants, and explorers
Are within this blood,
Within this history,
When we include
we find ourselves.

~AFTER DOM HÉLDER CÂMARA

This necklace as beautiful as a dream,
Tooth, husk, bead, skin,
Silent in the thick forest,
A prayer before the sacrifice,
The bow, the arrow, the howl.

~AFTER A TRADITIONAL CUBAN SAYING

I have no brakes,
So make my horn louder.

[. . .]

~AFTER ROBERTO JUARROZ

Light winks at me,
I blink back,
It goes like that,
I can take just so much at a time.

~AFTER PABLO NERUDA

At the beginning, mother and light are a single entity,
In the middle, a thousand thousand refractions,
In the end, a luminous heart.

*First line quotations taken from *Revelations: Latin American Wisdom for Every Day*, by Danielle and Olivier Föllmi, publisher: Harry N. Abrams, Inc., 2006

BARAKA'S MOUTH

Baraka's mouth, asymmetrical and syncopated,
jagged and jazzed,
a working garage mouth with the gritty tools to get under the hood
and get the engine going again,
it is a gigging mouth set with the machinery of the craft,
it is a working jackhammer mouth,
chipped and scarred,
a mouth that knows the pavement and how to crack it.

Baraka's primordial mouth is volcanic,
untouched, unshaped, and unruly,
incisors that cut through the crap,
an under bite that gets under the skin,
he has bitten off more than can be chewed
and he has had to cut a few to get the job done.

Baraka's teeth are bad for good reason,
he passes venom twice through his calcium gate-mouth—
once to get a taste,
and to set the record straight,
poisons take their toll,
he chomps at the iron-hard bit that has "we the people" gagged,
harnessed and obsessed with the obedient consumer lockstep,
and Amiri's teeth bear the scars of the battle,
they are veterans, crippled and broken,
whose brave work sheds grace upon thee.

Baraka screams through the corridors of institutionalized racism
and greed,
"Let me chew on that,"
and he does—wisely, thoroughly,
sacrificing his lips and tongue and teeth till he gets to the core.

[. . .]

He takes bites out of the steely gray glass sky-scratchers that corporate
America worships as the temples of commerce
and spits them back as compassionate rage,
tagging his bone-crushing mastications with
"Be a spirit, Be a spirit, Be a spirit."

I smile for you, Amiri Baraka,
when I see you open your mouth and talk.
I smile when I hear you shout wide open
with those damn obvious teeth that testify to decades
of truth-telling.
Amiri Baraka, I smile for you,
and with you.

BE BEATRICE

Beatrice was there at the frozen final ring of the Inferno
To calm Dante's heart and feet
So he could take the last steps of his ordeal
Into the fresh life the hellish journey had made possible.
Her beatific smile was nothing more than a tiny upward turn at the
    corners of her lips,
Wide eyes, relaxed shoulders, slow breath, full face forward to greet
    the world-weary poet,
Nothing of the Siren that he so often conjured,
Nothing of the innocent that broke his heart with her pale grace,
Nothing of the sweat, the moans, the pleading, or quaking voice,
Only her full face forward, eyes open, smiling to calm him through
    this last passage.

Tonight, it is cold.
A February rain drives sideways and noisy against my window,
The flag across the way at the village hall is drenched and sagging,
A lone car moves slowly down the street,
Its headlights beam far into the sleet.

Take my hand,
Cradle my head,
Hold me against your breast,
Breathe along with my breath,
Rock me this night across the barren plains of my longing.
Be Beatrice, be Beatrice.

ENTANGLEMENT

ENTANGLEMENT

Now that the scientists have caught up with us,
will love catch on like the hundredth
monkey with the sweet potato at the beach?
We knew from the beginning that entanglement
was the only efficient way forward;
the elegance and ease, the instantaneous transmission,
the recognition from afar.

Somewhere in Pasadena, locked in a research lab
bare but for a candle, two solitary souls sit facing one another
in silence,
experimenting with the new technology that says
what happens here can happen there,
when I move, you move,
when you move, I move,
we are connected.

Fool's Proof

It is a known fact that human beings are 2/3 water and 1/3 matter,
or 1/3 imagination,
or is it 2/3 imagination and 1/3 desire,
or equal parts bone and blood
and nothing more.
An elegant equation answers the puzzle.
The solution contains a changeability quotient calculated from the
    sum of the tides
multiplied by the chromatics of autumn leaves.
Only those who dress in ribbons and bells can master this
    mathematics,
no reasonable person would ever try,
common people lose their minds in the labyrinth of its proof,
our eyes glaze over contemplating the inscrutable symbols and
    squiggles of the line.
Only fools can walk on the water of this unstable symmetry.
Only fools fall in love.

RECIPE FOR BLOOD

Like wine, it can be made,
the ingredients are common,
but the effort is such
that few take the time,
for love is hard work.
This blood-type is the rarest,
it is not born in the marrow
but carefully cultivated
from the fruits that grow
in the fields of the heart.
The recipe calls for time and courage,
the simple ingredients must sit together
and seep courageously into each other
to exchange their flavors,
and slowly blend their tastes
into a new tongue-color,
the burgundy wine bouquet
of human love.

Man-made blood flows invisibly
through its co-creators
across oceans and mountains;
even the valley of the shadow of death
does not dam its determination.
This blood is invincible
to all illnesses
but neglect.

So be your brother's keeper,
be your sister's keeper,
for this blood is the true wine,
and when we are drunk with its flavor
we stumble upon the smooth foot-grooved stones
that pave the path of wisdom.

XTC

o
u n i
r
2 b

u n i
r
2 b
2 4 t
n t 4 2

OK?

y
u r d c
4 i

o
i m c n
u n i
r 2 b
n
y
f u r c n 2
b 2
i n u

i c u
n u n i
r 2 b n
xtc

MULTIVERSE

1.

This universe started with a big bang at a Niagara Falls motel,
a kiss, a caress, a gasp,
the insistent flippy swim of a sperm to an egg,
twinning mitosis,
tadpole, amphibian, fetus in Mother's sea,
birth, breath, breast,
creatureliness,
instincts,
clan, culture, companions, creations,
questions
into the mystery.

2.

The universe started with a small flash at a Niagara Falls motel
(we can make this part up, so why not?),
space/time emanating in all directions,
spreading, speeding up and out from that hot spot,
all hydrogen and helium
and then the 2% we are;
pots and pans in the sink,
unmade beds,
magicians and heretics.

[. . .]

3.

Gravity and attraction,
galaxy formation,
stellar furnaces burning,
churning out the periodic table proton by proton,
the incidental planets with their peculiarities;
their distance to their sun, their orbits, elemental compositions,
    atmospheres,
their infinite particular manifestations,
all the there and thens,
all the here and nows.

4.

This universe and the universe are entwined as a double helix,
Take one away and the other ceases to function,
The universe has made the mind,
The mind has made the universe.

5.

Space-time flows through solar storms and the bones of this body,
The atoms in these fingers and the pixel-scribed words they set on the
    screen
are saturated with radiation from the instant of cosmic beginning,
These very words, spoken aloud in this warm room,
echo into infinity.

6.

Let every poet study the stars,
let every astronomer be a lyricist,
let's start again,
let's return to the knotty questions,
to the straight facts,
to the fractal flux
where this universe and the universe are one;
somewhere in this joining,
may revelation begin.

How the Making Happens

Emma, 3 years old, dips her finger into a puddle at the river's edge,
she swizzles it around and around,
delighting in the bubbles and eddies she has conjured.
Me, I stare at my draining tub,
the indifferent flatness of the bath water whirls into a vortex
and disappears.

I confess a guilty fascination
when I click into *weather.com*
and see the chaotic imprint of our planetary origins
in the elegant, furious spinning of tornadoes
that tear through Missouri towns,
and the hurricanes that beat Puerto Rico to a pulp.

This swirling,
this drawing into solidity,
was/is how the making happens,
like the shaman at the fire stirring her conjuring pot,
making the potion that creates
all that is real
all that is imagined
all of it,
all of us,
made from one effect of gravity
or another.

YOUR FOOTSTEPS

The barometer has gone through the ceiling,
storms gather, burst and go
and return,
leaves and branches litter the street,
everywhere there are echoes.
I have given my center of gravity over to you,
nothing roots me anymore,
the slightest breeze and I'm toppled to the ground,
it's where I belong anyway,
my ear to the pavement listening for your footsteps
running to me through the night.

WANTED TO KNOW

You said you wanted to know,
I bit down on the hard truth
that lying would be worse.
I told you and
your eyes hardened, crumbled;
an ocean rose between us,
you are somewhere I can't see,
the horizon is empty,
my heart beats with the heavy bangs
of one who has momentarily lost his kid at the beach,
stranded,
the crashing surf drowns all songs.

THIS FURY

This is slow-cooked fury,
furnace fury,
fever fury,
fury that fills to the skin,
a tiny pinprick makes it burst.

This is back-of-the-neck-like-a-hammer-shaft fury,
nostrils chugging like a locomotive fury,
fury that sounds alarms,
that designs nightmares,
that burns.

This fistful of fury leaves nail marks,
pounds the table,
shakes at the moon,
punches the palm.

This fury writhes through me
like a Chinese New Year dragon
animated by a ward of convulsing chimps.
This fury is a volcanic spout from the molten core of creation;
it spits curses from the dead languages of the earth.

BETWEEN US

There is nothing between us,
Thin air, light, not much else.
I kneel before this empty altar and wait
Till the grammar of longing speaks,
Nouns and verbs fall from my eyes.
This moment cannot be contained in the abstraction of language,
No matter how poetic;
It is just the silence, the gaze,
And the ineffable vocabulary of every quiet thing
Between us.

ABOVE, BELOW, IN BETWEEN

THERE IS A UNIVERSE GROWING IN MY BASEMENT

There is a universe growing in my basement
designed by drunken butterflies and blind astronomers,
unseen forces jiggle everything,
dust and magnetism,
elemental matter and photons,
nebulae and mitochondria,
all expanding, radiating out
toward the horizons of destiny.

I Speak for the Living Earth

I speak for the living earth,
for the subterranean species,
for the highfliers,
the elements,
for basalt and argon,
hydrogen, iron,
for a sightless creature deep within a cave.

I speak for the north wind on the Wyoming plains,
for the shale fields of Kilimanjaro,
the blue ice of the glacier,
the gold blood of the volcano.
I speak for the micro-world,
for the spores and seeds,
the pollen of a rose.

I speak for the four-legged,
the two-legged, the squirmers, and crawlers,
for the leopard and hound,
the python and giraffe.
I speak for the rivers,
for swift-churning currents,
for the gentle mountain spring.

I speak for the shifting surface of the planet,
for roiling magma,
the explosive eruption, the changes.
I speak for the canyons,
for what is told in their cliffs,
for the sound of the emptiness,
for the birds,
the ibis and crow,
the crane and swallow.

I speak for the night,
for the eyes that open,
the dew that falls.
I speak for the sea,
for the crust of salt on a shell.

I speak for the infinite horizon,
for the unknown,
for the unfound,
the unborn,
the threatened,
the endangered,
the extinct.

I speak for the seasons,
for the birth of all things,
for the death of all things,
for the trees,
the willow and birch,
the linden and oak.

I speak for morning on the ridge,
noon at a desert oasis,
dusk at the shore,
night in the singing forest.

I speak for the mist that rises from the waterfall,
for the stillness of the hummingbird,
the turbulence of the sea,
the mountain avalanche,
sunlight on the river.

[. . .]

I speak for the rain,
for the storm,
the rising water,
the hurricane.

I speak for the desert in spring,
for forsythia's first bloom,
for the plump berries of mid-July,
for the last red leaf,
for the ice-glazed branch against the deep blue sky.

I speak for the mountain peaks,
for the silence,
the starry night.

I speak for the four directions,
for the ground beneath our feet,
for the fruit we eat,
for color, and all we touch,
for the fragrance of honeysuckle.
I speak for the relation of all things,
I speak for the miracle of being,

I speak for the living earth.

SILENT DIALECT

In a maple,
saw in hand,
foot in a crook,
back firm against the trunk,
gripping a four-inch branch,
rough ridges of bark pressing into my palm,
up there,
in an instant,
a leaf speaks,
    sunlight reveals the network of veins,
    the shine of new spring green,
    the fractal symmetry in its jagged form,
the silent dialect of wonder.

WHITE DOTS/BLACK VOID

The vexing jumble of white dots and black void
tonight sheds its absurdity like a skin,
with you and your lens and green laser pointer
I can tolerate the chaos,
relationships become obvious,
rams, fish, bulls, tea kettles, and ladles
assemble from the mess,
connecting lines become visible,
the steamy center of the Milky Way pours
from the spout of Sagittarius,
the arms of the galaxy reach away from our sun,
Jupiter's moons string to the east,
Polaris is in line with the Little Dipper,
Andromeda hovers as a dollop of thin gauze below Cassiopeia,
all of it
clear as day.

ECLIPSE

Neither Nostradamus nor Edgar Cayce could have predicted
last night's full lunar eclipse—
their visions reached just so far.
At first she was bold,
sailing even-keeled across the heavens, keeping watch,
then she was touched,
stained slowly, like ink bled into a napkin
till all her light slipped off but for a slim crescent at the bottom of her
    bowl,
like the eyelid of a sleeping child,
and then even that shut,
so that she disappeared,
vanished at the height of her radiance like a fairy princess
run off between courses at the ball,
determined to live a life of adventure.
It has taken astronomers and mathematicians
squinting through their scopes,
wrestling gnarly calculus,
buoyed and propelled by the accumulated knowledge of a hundred
    generations
to know that she'd return,
once again gathered in her silver silks
to continue her vigilant sojourn of the night.

TIDES

A phantom ache haunts me,
Like a twin gone missing at the beach,
Each anxious instant is a drop of gray,
When you are by my side the turbulence of the sea is a gift,
When you are not, storm clouds fill my ears and descend,
spreading thunder to the crevices of my anatomy.

Skin of hazel mist,
Hair of night horizon,
Eyes framed by the trails of shooting stars...
With these words I work to conjure you.

Tides rise and fall,
Each season has its charm,
Every phase of the moon illuminates.

STARFISH

White sand, an underwater desert of rolling dunes,
contours, hips,
topography, body form at the bottom of the sea.

Shafts of gold light, flitting, shifting, dropping,
a holographic curtain of falling gold,
light blades cutting through the saltwater.

Floating on the surface in thirty feet of clear Caribbean water,
swimming out to the island reef,
tasting the sea,
eyes open to all this.

A gold starfish
big as a dinner plate on the white sand,
shafts of light, another one, and another,
six, eight, dozens of stars,
shafts of light, white sand,
another and another,
suspended between the golden under-sea galaxy below
and the celestial one above,
one of five-fingered creatures,
one of boiling suns,
the human mind in between.

Eyes open to all this.

BangFlash

Space, time, matter, and energy lived in a crowded crib at the corner
    of mystery street,
limbs and lips entwined at the busy spot,
as singular as lovers dissolved by mutual moan and gaze,
they'd hung out this way since,
well...

Flash,
the new universe was/is born,
a nanosecond old she cries and sound comes into being,
stretches, and there is movement,
lifts her head, curiosity,
places a hand, exploration,
shuffles a knee, expansion,
Crawling out in/to what she creates
Millimeter by sacred millimeter.

Space-time grows out to meet herhimthey
fourteen billion years old/young, your choice.
She
keeps
on
going
growing in all directions at once,
each galaxy moving away from every other galaxy,
And then, dear lovers,
There is you.

INTO THE NIGHT AIR

-after Walt Whitman

When I heard the learn'd astronomer,
when the board filled with the arcs and symbols of the craft,
when invited to enter the idea-world beyond all I see,
when I opened the eye of my mind to the heavens
for the first time,
with the astronomer curious
and quiet before the mysteries,
how my heart quickened and my thoughts raced,
till rising and gliding out, I wandered off by myself
into the night-air,
to gaze upon the brilliant puzzle of diamonds in the sky,
perfect in their silent beckoning
for understanding.

LIFE CODE

I will surround myself with the history of life on earth,
A fossilized crab caught pulling itself from the sands,
Petrified dinosaur bones,
The massive skull of an extinct turtle,
Vertebrae, wide as an albatross's wingspan, from a great blue whale.

I will surround myself with the documents of biodiversity
To place evolution at my fingertips,
To touch the branches of the animal kingdom,
To allow my imagination to rummage up the tree of life,
To feel the grain of the leopard's spotted fur,
The smooth arc of the mammoth's tusk,
The ridged curvature of the water buffalo's horn.

I will surround myself
With skeletons and pelts,
Taxidermy specimens, and pin-trays
Displaying the fluorescence of beetles,
Scarabs and formations of marching tarantulas.

I will display my treasures
In dust-tight cases,
On pedestals, common hooks, and custom stands,
The polar bear shall lie before the fire.

Alone in my dead-silent study
The species will speak to me
In hisses, squeals,
Grunts, and mellifluous birdsongs,
Each voice claiming a part within the harsh, chaotic beauty.

In the corner,
Suspended between a giraffe's skull
And a rhino's jawbone,
Will be a human stripped of flesh and blood,
His eye sockets vacant,
Shocked and speechless at his placement
Within the beastly catalog of creation.

THE NEW GREEN

The old forest is scorched and fallen.
A field of charred totems tower into the sky.
The new green grows wide and free.
Shoots rising up out of the moist soil, ferns unfurling.
With us or without us,
The old forest relinquishes,
Her seeds are everywhere opening to the sun,
Reaching to the blue,
The burnt forest recedes.
With us or without us,
The new green grows wide and free.

SEND YOURSELF INTO THE AIR

Read your biography in the activities of insects,
the hovering dragonfly,
the pollen-soaked bee,
the solitary spider in her silver web.

Send yourself into the air as a yellow bird,
the river speaks your native tongue,
the double rainbow confirms,
the rippling pink clouds at dusk say
"Call her, she needs you."

Every mundane thing is a poem in hiding,
the deciphering touch of your imagination unpacks the moment,
coincidences are temple bells,
the sound of the drum is filled with silence,
silence is a symphony,
nothing is solely as it appears,
every beauty is part of a sacred text
written on a parchment of wonder.

SOCIAL ECOLOGY

1.

Patriarchal hierarchical
power system
dominates
decimates
this man-made schism
this barbarism
slices our ecological nature
from our social nature.

It's the system
the neurotically, compulsively expand-or-die system
like a psychotic ouroboros
a hoarding, misogynistic, and paranoid system
that shits where it eats
Othering
every
other
thing
A dominion of spewing toxic factories and pesticide-ridden farms
As if growth were an end in itself
You've got no home but bank vaults and the golden toilet you call a
    throne.

2.

The beast is out of the cage,
devour or be devoured,
endless growth,
endless consumption
feckless,
reckless,
fuck this.

Corporations peddle ecological mirages
with *think green,*
be green,
do green,
all the while raking in the green.
The grass grows greener,
but meaner,
chromosomal aberrations rise through the food chain,
just watch a three-legged frog hop.

From the university of the streets a message to
the university of the cheats
this systemic arrogance is willful,
this myopic gluttony is a choice,
imperialism is doin' us,
it's ruinous,
to all of us.

BACK TO THE BEGINNING

MY BECKONING

Forces of creation
Here is my beckoning.
Smooth the gnarled receptors of my old brain,
Redirect the molecules of your enchantments,
Prepare me for a surprise,
Bring on something;
I will close my eyes,
Inhale, surrender,
And direct my breath.

TRAJECTORY

A train whistles in the distance,
the station attendant switches the lamp on,
heats a pot of coffee,
peers down the track to check on the signals,
the rails have shifted,
the lights are green,
all is good.

The train stops, opens for its cargo,
the engineer drinks his cup,
they chat about the 49ers game and the wind coming from the west.
A bell rings, the load is done,
a handshake between the two,
and off again down the track.

The absurdity of toy trains on a circular track
charms children and monks;
everyone else knows that trains only make sense
in their trajectory.

THIS NEW WORLD

I have stepped off the four-square map
into an uncharted opening
beyond the continents and the canyons of the sea.

My world was flat,
now it is upside down/inside out,
I'm falling I'm flying I'm suspended
in a kaleidoscope of color, form, scent, wind, possibility,
it is all mind/heart/soul in this new world.

I throw my arms, palms up, into the air,
I close my eyes,
I drop my head back,
I breathe in deeply through my nostrils.
With this gesture my body beckons;
the answer I get is a sigh.

I've stepped into the unknown
beneath my left foot is truth,
beneath my right foot is trust.
I claim this territory in the name of love.

THE MIRACLE OF OUR NEAR SPACE

Hiking up the desert hill at dusk, stepping from one garnet and sand-hued rock to the next so as not to trample the carpet of yellow and purple flowers that forms a delicate living sea, so as to get to a vista of the Joshua Trees against the glowing horizon, so as to remember that this life is a moment, that this world is the miracle of our near space, that the setting sun is a lyric that gets us through the disorientation of night, that a witness sharpens the pain of magnificence, that love opens the doors of perception, and that what is seen at dusk on a blooming desert hill can change us forever.

CRAZY WOMAN CREEK CANYON

For two thousand feet the path swooped and curled
along the bounding stream.
Crimson-yellow grasses rose to meet my fingertips,
a red squirrel blessed the day,
wildflowers made my eyes widen,
sage was in the air.
I laid a pair of stick spirits in the sand seeming to walk into
and out of the earth at the same time;
this was my mark, the transient proof that I had been there.

With every step the canyon cliffs rose higher,
guarding my journey into the deep,
so that the silence could speak,
so that the river could reveal the wisdom of flowing truth,
so that nature could have her way with me.
I lived a lifetime that day.

On the Crazy Woman Creek Canyon trail,
all things are measured by their luminosity.
It ends with a short pine bridge like the hyphen at the end of this
    sentence—
It just ends there.
As if the purpose of all that traveling was simply to stand
suspended over the timeless flow,
there is no path beyond,
no blazes, no signs, no footprints,
no precedents.

EAGLE CLIFF

Stuck and holding on,
a bloody knuckle grip into the Minnewaska granite,
a toehold with the right foot,
the left on a one-inch ledge,
spread-eagled thirty-five feet above
rock shards that slid off this mountain
before sound was born on earth,
I am scaling Eagle Cliff alone,
when a bee buzzes my ear
and returns again and again
in tight chaotic orbits.
Why am I here?
Going back is impossible,
...there...a rotted pine shrub,
barely within reach of my left fingertips...
I grab for
it, seems to snap even before I touch
it, falls out of my hand to the rocks
(below, I was immortal; now I'm
not on terra firma anymore,
thoughts of my
kids don't have to prove to themselves that they are young
forever)

shoulder elbow wrist digits jerk away from the mountain
my right hand digs deeper into its crack hips
and thighs push against the wall I arch my spine in a convulsion.

In this infinite moment
oblivion invades my lungs
leaves the etchings of her claws
on the chambers of my heart
as a warning.

Body World

I've taken off my skin searching for it,
I've removed my eyes from their sockets,
I've removed my testes from their sac,
I've laid every organ on the table,
left no tissue unturned,
no structure unexamined,
I know it's here somewhere,
tucked between the ulna and radius,
floating along the channels of my bloodstream,
nesting in the folds of my brain?
I stripped down to my bones,
dissolved them with all sorts of solutions,
but nothing,
still the song quietly sings through my body world,
lyrical as the virgin landscape,
melodious,
composed,
intact.

KILIMANJARO

What is seen by the naked eye
From the steep slope of Kilimanjaro on a moonless night
Is the simple truth.
It comes in silent awestruck breaths,
It comes at once,
Like Plato's protagonist I wandered out of the cave into the light
To see, and know, that the bounds of my homeland were no more
What they once were,
That I had been living in a smaller fiction,
That the location of my life, of this life,
Was resituated into a grander cosmic scale,
And that my home is a brilliant spiral of one billion stars and planets
    dancing around themselves
Within the ballroom of the universe,
The arms of the home galaxy reaching away, and back again,
Gyrating, generating,
Spinning, shining, moving,
And me in stop-time, jaw dropped, craning my neck to the sight,
Breathless, silent,
and relieved.

KRISHNA'S RICE

The statue of Krishna travels in a crate of rice
On his journey from Madras to Madrid.
Millions of grains closely pack the saint;
They sleep upon his eyelids,
Nuzzle in his armpits,
Dream with him of timelessness and courage.
When he arrives, Krishna's legs won't take him to the river,
His fingers won't feel the breeze,
His flute will be silent,
But the rice is fragrant,
At the ashram devotees celebrate with a feast.
Each grain holds the memory of water, soil, light,
The touch of a human hand.
Each grain holds the kernel of nourishment
Needed to do the work of being.

To Breathe and Breathe

This consciousness of time
that brings the death angel to stand upon our shoulder
makes us human.
Sparrows alight on branches, then fly till they fly no more,
wild turkeys roam and peck and stay close to the pack
till their last,
oh, to be the tiny bird or the wizened one,
innocent and with a single mind,
oh, to relinquish the minor-god status bestowed with this wide-
   awake mortality,
to live where there are no clocks, only the turning galaxy
and beyond,
to direct imagination into eternity,
to breathe and breathe till we breathe no more.

SPINS THE WHEEL

Somewhere in the cosmos, ninety years old,
she sits at the dining room table
as quiet as a constellation,
teaspoon by teaspoon her memory disperses into oblivion.

Playing Whirly Word on her iPad,
in the jumble of letters she finds
"air, hair, chair";
she spins the wheel again for a new scramble.
For five hours a day
this is the entirety
of my mother's fleeting world.

She'd been in Saigon in '68
Trekked the Siberian tundra
Dove the Great Barrier Reef
Shopped Parisienne couture.

Spins the wheel
"ill, till, still"
For the thousandth time she tells me
"Life is a dream."

She'd partied in Ibiza
Skied the Italian Alps
Rolled on Ecstasy
Bowed to her guru in India.

Spins the wheel,
"ace, pace, space"
"No, really,
Life really is a dream."

[. . .]

In four billion years Homegalaxy will
collide with Andromeda,
but the apparent catastrophe
won't trouble even a single blade of grass,
won't dither whatever bio-cyber consciousness survives this infinite
   cycle of extinctions.

They will approach,
they will interact with spectacular gravitational dynamics,
billions of stars will draw together,
two becoming one,
the way that first true lover's caress
changed everything
forever

Spins the wheel
      "dear, *Madre*, dream."

Rest, My Warriors

-for Gabriel García Márquez

By the shore you shall sleep,
by midnight I will come.

By the shore you shall sleep,
with the choral hum of the waves at your ear,
by midnight I will come.

By the shore you shall sleep,
beneath a blue-black blanket sequined with galaxies and shooting
   stars, clasped by the crescent moon,
by midnight I will come.

By the shore you shall sleep,
breathing the free winds of the earth,
by midnight I will come.

By the shore you shall sleep,
upon soft sands and tiny treasures washed up out of the aqua-world,
by midnight I will come.

By the shore you shall sleep,
where water and dirt kiss open-mouthed, and all is moist,
by midnight I will come.

You are within my sight and I watch you,
Your light dazzles my iris and intoxicates,
I take you in like honeyed wine.
I know what you have done,
I will come to you before this day is through.

Rest,
by the shore you shall sleep,
by midnight I will come.

DEAD SEA

I want to tell you everything I know about death, the finality
that comes in moments toward tomorrow, the confusion,
the relief that what we intuit is true, that life
ends in death, as simple as that, that what burns
is the fire of incomplete loving, that complete loving
belongs only to angels, the rest of us must moan
and grieve alone, and in the company of the lost,
that the community of the tearful fills an ocean we can float
upon, a Dead Sea, where together we bob and sink till
we reach the sands of memory, or distraction,
or wisdom.

ISABELA

Six-month-old Isabela swaddled in her father's muscular arms;
I'd cradled him when he was newborn,
now he gazes into his daughter's eyes,
lost in the miraculous moment.

"Where did she come from?" I ask.
A sly smile overtakes his face.
"No, where did she really come from?"
His grin dissolves into blank confusion.
"What do you mean?" he says.

"I mean, where do stories like this begin?"

THE ROSE OF MERCY

Tío Victor wrapped in the cloak of senility
Inching toward the oblivion,
Disturbing the bedsheets,
In a riverside home,
Wide-eyed and asleep,
Dreaming in grimaces and fists
He arranges the affairs of his soul
Between the quiet shores of forgetting
And the tempests of his midnight rage.
The nurses and attendants tolerate his ranting
Calm him with cold compresses, warm hands,
The knowing voices of tenderness,
Angels singing him to the gate.

At his bedside, holding his gnarled fingers in the palm of my hand,
I hum "Old Man River"
     He just keeps rolling along...
The life-long anthem with which he prepared himself for these very
   days,
Watching Tío Victor sleep slack-jawed,
The gaping hole,
The heaving breath,
The leaving,
The holding on.

Tío Victor sits up
Points to me to get my pen
Paper on the dresser,
Write:
Cultivo, rosa, blanca,
Words, random, fragments, I write them, these sea-leavings washed
   up from the depths of his unconscious mind.

Cultivo la rosa blanca
La rosa blanca
Cultivo la rosa blanca
En junio como en enero,

Writing,
What is this? Writing,
His gaze is upon me, ancient eyes sharpened,
Struggling, drawing the words slowly up from the deep, near-dry well
   of his imagination,
The heavy lifting yields scant spoonfuls,
Hard work for a frail 92-year-old man at the crossroads.

Para el amigo sincero
        Word by word
        Phrase by phrase
        Repeating line by line
        Over and over...
Cultivo la rosa blanca
En junio como en enero
Para el amigo sincero
Que me da su mano franca

Y para el cruel,
El cruel,
Que me arranca—arranca
El corazón, corazón
Y para el cruel que me arranca
El corazón con que vivo—vivo,
Cardos ni ortigas cultivo
Cultivo la rosa blanca
Cultivo la rosa blanca
Blanca.

[. . .]

When it was done, when he knew I had it all down right,
Tío Victor closed his eyes, shifted to the side and fell asleep.
I went home that night to set his sonnet to music,
Unaware that *La Rosa Blanca* was Cuban poet José Martí's most
    famous lyric,
Breathing into Tío Victor's final gift to me,
The everlasting perfume of a rose whose essence is mercy,
Whose scent remains.

GATHERING WATERS

Let there be a song of praise for the gathering waters at this place.
Let there be a song of praise for the nameless tributaries,
and a song for the Seven Seas.
Let there be a song of praise for the currents that pan the distant
  streambeds of the earth
to deposit their treasures at our feet.
Let there be a song of praise for bracing Canadian springs,
for the Yangtze and the Mississippi Delta,
for Hudson Bay and Harlem River.
Let there be a song of praise for the convergence of salt and sweet,
each flowing into each other,
white-capped and tumultuous,
making something new in the brackish womb of their joining.
Let there be a song of praise for this stirring of turbulent histories.
Let there be a song of praise for this brimming liquid now-moment.
Let there be a joyous song,
an anthem,
for this blessed confluence of longing.

ACKNOWLEDGMENTS

IN GRATITUDE

This book came to be with the support and inspiration of many friends, teachers, poets, and musicians:

Sekou Sundiata, Juan Mobili, Lissa Kiernan, Jimmy Santiago Baca, Juan Felipe Hererra, Miguel Algarín, Kim Peter Kovac, Robert A. Johnson, Maxine Greene, Carolyn Kenny, Clive Robbins, Ernest Becker, Joseph Campbell, Jose Maria Marquez, Jake Sokolov-Gonzalez, Raina Sokolov-Gonzalez, Daniel Kelly, Steve Gorn, Ev Mann, Harvey Sorgen, Álvaro Domene, Luke Keller, Lupe Echevarria, Richard Ouelette, John DiMartino, Erik Lawrence, Willie Martinez, Larry Harlow, Wilson,"Chembo" Corniel, Miles, Trane, Billie, Dizzy, Jimi, and the pantheon of sonic deities who have blessed my ears and soul.

Special thanks to Cindy Hochman of "100 Proof" Copyediting Services, whose editorial input was essential to this book.

PUBLICATION CREDITS

"The Miracle of Our Near Space" appeared in *First Literary Review-East,* March 2022.

EARLY PRAISE FOR SOUNDINGS

Soundings—alarms and the *radiating out* of a new consciousness, an earth and cosmos in totality, a notebook of lives, ancestors, praise, familia and their reverberations and intrinsic pathways into and for each other. A book of chants and enlightenments, home spirit and space particles as One. As Gonzalez says in one of his poems, *recognitions and transmissions*—this is at the core of this collection. That is, to recognize all things and to live in the constant exchange of each. This is a most necessary voice and text, concerned with a profound, inspiring view of humanity—an investigation into our expansiveness, our magnificent reach into incredible songs of Being never imagined, yet to be lived. Here are the maps for a self of earth and cosmos interconnections, breath, existence and thought—for the new thinker, traveler, philosopher. *Bravo, brava!*

—Juan Felipe Herrera
Poet Laureate of the United States, Emeritus

Welcome to the birth of a poet! Of course, David Gonzalez has always been a poet; it shines through his work as a storyteller, musician, actor. But now, with *Soundings*, David the poet takes center stage, and what we find is poetry tough as the sidewalks of Nueva York, sweet as breeze in Boricua. We hear his own voice—*autentico nuyoriqueño*—where *El Barrio, el finger-tip grip onto the American dream,/ where half the streets open wide to the horizon,/ and the other half are dead ends,/ y donde el ritmo no tiene fin,/ and the groove is deep. Soundings* is a must for libraries where the groove is deep, where the rhythm never ends.

—Bob Holman
poet and founder of the Bowery Poetry Club

I come from saints and sinners, each left their mark says David Gonzalez in one of his poems and what may appear like an unproven declaration to invite you into his *Soundings*, becomes a statement of fact as soon as you walk through this book's pages.

Actually, David is more than the unwitting descendant from holy and dark tribes, he has their eyes, and what he sees through them, forged in the fires of his poems, is this life of ours, a river of glories and regrets, navigated by his relatives and their spirited voices. A diary of sorts of what imperfect and impeccable souls taught him, and he shares intelligently and generously with us.

Gonzalez knows that *entanglement was the only efficient way forward,* how else a poet, even as talented as he is, could even begin to tell the truth about our world? That is his gift to us: to pull you like a moon in love with tides to celebrate our humanity, knowing full well he had to embrace *the grief necessary to make this earth of troubles/ into a home.*

These are the words of an unabashed soul whose birth had his *big bang at a Niagara Falls motel,/ a kiss, a caress, a gasp,* and we ought to be grateful for that motel where these *Soundings* began, grateful for their kiss, their caress, their gasp.

—Juan Pablo Mobili, poet, author of *Contraband*

Let there be a song of praise pleads the protagonist in "Gathering Waters" from *Soundings,* the inaugural poetry collection from decorated storyteller David Gonzalez. His exhilarating collection generously complies, turning up the radio and opening the windows wide on a wild-eyed road trip ranging from Cuba to Puerto Rico (*I come from the graceful trajectories of quarks and uncertainty, I come from the snap of a finger long, long ago*) to New York's Spanish Harlem, aka El Barrio (*the magnificent location of our mortal unwinding*). Spending time with this Nuyorican poet's work is akin to a fantastical gathering around a global firepit, a combustion of the magical tales, songs, and conversations that might ensue. With a voracious appetite for all of life's shadings as well as its soundings, imbued with a heartfelt sense of the sacred for both family and place, Gonzalez waxes Whitmanesque as he enters the canon—effusive, exuberant, erudite—*every mundane thing a poem in hiding,* all senses on fire.

—Lissa Kiernan, author of *The Whispering Wall*

ABOUT THE AUTHOR

 David Gonzalez is a storyteller, playwright, and performer whose poetry has been featured at *Lincoln Center's Out-of-Doors Festival*, Bill Moyers' documentary *Fooling with Words*, and NPR's *All Things Considered*, and at universities and performing arts centers across the country. *Oh Hudson,* a long-form piece, was commissioned by the Empire State Plaza Performing Arts Center to commemorate the Quadricentennial of Hudson's exploration. *City of Dreams,* a spoken-word/Latin jazz project, commissioned by The University of Maryland and La MaMa, has toured throughout the U.S. David wrote the opera libretto for *Rise for Freedom*, as well as numerous plays, including *The Man of the House* (commissioned by the Kennedy Center for the Performing Arts); *Mariel*, an Afro-Cuban musical (commissioned by Cincinnati Playhouse in the Park); *The Boy Who Could Sing Pictures*, and many more. Mr. Gonzalez has toured widely throughout the U.S. and abroad. He received his doctorate in Music Therapy from New York University and has garnered numerous awards and commissions. He is a Joseph Campbell Foundation Fellow, has extensive experience supporting communities through the arts, and is a proud recipient of the International Performing Arts for Youth "Lifetime Achievement Award for Sustained Excellence."

David was the founder and Artistic Director of the Rockland County Storytelling Festival (1996–2006). For eight seasons he was the host of New York Kids (1992–2000), a high-energy live radio program on New York Public Radio WNYC-FM, where fun, fast-paced creativity and social relevance for children was the mission.

Gonzalez's professional life began scholastically in the field of Music Therapy, where he earned undergraduate, master's, and doctorate degrees. For twenty years he worked at social service sites throughout the New York City area with disabled and medically ill children, as well as adult psychiatric patients. The joining of art and human services set the context for meaning in his life and shaped the artistic vision that continues to drive his creative work today.

He has published two books for young readers that are available on Amazon: *Tío Jose and the Singing Trees* and *Tito and the Bridge Brigade.*

David lives in the Hudson Valley region of New York State.

ABOUT THE POETRY BOX®

The Poetry Box, a boutique publishing company in Portland, Oregon, provides a platform for both established and emerging poets to share their words with the world through beautiful printed books and chapbooks.

Feel free to visit the online bookstore (thePoetryBox.com), where you'll find more titles including:

The Weight of Clouds by Cathy Cain

This Is the Lightness by Rachel Barton

Earthwork by Kristin Berger

Cosmology of Heaven & Hell by Michael Waterson

Songs from Back-in-the-Back by Marcia B. Loughran

This Conversation by Christopher Bogart

Late Fall Bucolics by Anne Coray

Sophia & Mister Walter Whitman by Penelope Scambly Schott

A Nest in the Heart by Vivienne Popperl

What We Bring Home by Susan Coultrap McQuin

Contraband by Juan Pablo Mobili

Olympic by John L. Miller

Gaslight Opera by Gary Percesepe`

World Gone Zoom by David Belmont

Exchanging Wisdom by Christopher & Angelo Luna

and more . . .

www.ingramcontent.com/pod-product-compliance
Lightning Source LLC
La Vergne TN
LVHW011954160425
808840LV00013B/51